Printed in Great Britain

HOP
LIKE ME

Jean and Gareth
Adamson

ALBERT WHITMAN & Company – Chicago

Copyright © Jean Adamson 1972 · L.C. Catalog Card Number 72-79799
Published simultaneously in Canada by George J. McLeod Ltd · Toronto

Look at me. I am a frog.
Hop, hop, hop. Hop like me.

Hop like you, Frog?
I am much too big
to do that.

Look at me. I am a horse.
Trot, trot, trot. Trot like me.

Trot like you, Horse?
How could I,
without any legs?

Look at me.
I am a worm.
Wriggle, wriggle.
Wriggle like me.

Wriggle like you, Worm?
You come along with me.
I will show you something
much better than wriggling.

Look at me. I am a bird.
Fly, fly, fly. Fly like me.

Fly like you, Bird?
Oh, how I would love
to fly high in the sky.
But I have no wings.

Look at me. I am a hare.
Run, run, run. Run like me.

Run like you, Hare?
My tail and fins
are not made for running.

Look at me.
I am a fish.
Swim, swim, swim.
Swim like me.

Swim like you, Fish?
I tried to swim once,
but I sank.

Look at me.
I am a spider.
Crawl, crawl, crawl.
Crawl like me.

Crawl like you, Spider?
Come a little closer
and show me
just how you do it.